FINISHING LINE PRESS

www.finishinglinepress.com

The Blackened Blues

poems by

Sean Murphy

Finishing Line Press
Georgetown, Kentucky

The Blackened Blues

For my wife, Heather,
who showed me all the things I didn't know about love.

ACKNOWLEDGMENTS

"Charlie Parker's Premonition": *FIVE:2:ONE*
"Kurt Vonnegut's Cigarettes": *Blotterature*
"Billie Holiday's Deathbed": *Decolonial Passage*
"Liz Taylor's Talents": *Panoply*
"Joey Kocur's Fist": *Sport Literate*
"Himmler's First Blasphemy": *Exterminating Angel Press*
"Bud Powell's Brain," "Howlin' Wolf's Arena," and "Sun Ra's Spaceship":
    Sequestrum
"Charles Mingus's Miracle"and "Sonny Rollins's Bridge": *Burningword*
"Charles Bukowski's Bounty": *Linden Avenue*
"Private Pyle's Pain": The Good Men Project
"Roland Kirk's Dream," "John Coltrane's Cancer," and "Booker Little's
    Deliverance": *Jerry Jazz Musician*
"Shafi Hadi's Silence": *Empty Mirror*
"Henry Chinaski's Horses": *jmww*

Publisher: Leah Huete de Maines
Editor: Christen Kincaid
Graphic design by Morgan Ryan (morganryancreative.com) using a significantly
modified original photograph by Patrick Hendry (unsplash.com)
Author Photo courtesy of Paul Misencik

Order online: www.finishinglinepress.com
        also available on amazon.com

Author inquiries and mail orders:
Finishing Line Press
PO Box 1626
Georgetown, Kentucky 40324
USA

Table of Contents

Charles Bukowski's Bounty 1

Charles Mingus's Miracle 3

Charlie Parker's Premonition 5

Billie Holiday's Deathbed 6

Bud Powell's Brain 7

Howlin' Wolf's Arena 8

Sun Ra's Spaceship 9

Liz Taylor's Talents 10

Joey Kocur's Fist.. 11

Chef's Second Chance 12

Captain Ahab's Oil... 13

Himmler's First Blasphemy 14

Bill Cosby's Blindness 15

Trayvon's Last Meal 17

Tina Turner's Legs 18

Jimi Hendrix's Hair 19

Jake LaMotta's Rage.. 20

Private Pyle's Pain 21

Kurt Vonnegut's Cigarettes 22

Beethoven's Silent Consecration... 23

Richard Pryor's Flesh 24

Ornette Coleman's Question 25

Sonny Rollins's Bridge 26

Roland Kirk's Dream 27

Eric Dolphy's Death 28

Booker Little's Deliverance.. 29

John Coltrane's Cancer 30

Shafi Hadi's Silence.. 31

Henry Chinaski's Horses 34

Charles Bukowski's Bounty

You could write a poem about this:
That was the story of his life.

The story of his stories, something more
authentic than life, which is what Art can be.

Failure a half-empty amphitheater where ideas are born.

Anyone can orchestrate chaos but it takes guts
to own it, even if you can't describe or explain it.

Between spilled beers and bruised hands there's a question:
What kind of world would you create, even if you couldn't?

Take that mattress, out in the street, second-hand
salvation for those disinclined to inquire, but unafraid
to inherit; in this part of town everyone knows shit
you throw into a dumpster doesn't go there to die.
There's always someone hungrier or less happy, someone
who will not go quietly into that precarious night—
grateful to have the things you no longer need.

Those women were not unlike the poems and stories:
they were the gold you spun from the machine we call
Misfortune, or being brave enough to figure out you own time
even when you can't make money; money and time own you
unless you flip the script, sucking & fucking the sweetness
Life lets you steal when it's looking the other way.

Content to sleep or screw or imagine better realities, lying
on a sullied mattress, unworried by their stains or the untruths
they could tell, contaminating you in unintended ways, because
we share everything anyhow, the ugliness most of all.
And miserable men become mice scurrying away from that evidence,
scared to reconcile the ways we made these fictions of ourselves
in our own likeness way before the world ever got involved.

And that's why well-fed and wordless sheep pace silently inside
extravagant pens, erected to secure them from all the surprises
cops and cars and banks and bibles can't protect or serve.

Or prevent the moon from sweet-talking the tides to turn or the sun, setting without comment over shallow graves dug with dirty fingernails, bleeding insolently onto dry-cleaned suits: symphonies of all the seconds and cents spent, hoping to hide the sick and satisfied smile of a Universe that will throw all of us, ultimately, into immaculate recycling bins where, once we die, starving saints turn us into stories and poems.

Charles Mingus's Miracle

The thing about Charlie Mingus Jr.—who clattered
onto the scene like a grand piano in a punch bowl—
is that he also was young once. More than that, fate
made him endure indignities that make a street bum
look like Reagan's strapping young buck on food stamps,
savoring a T-bone. System so sullied even mobsters did
more than music critics, but you know, *that's entertainment.*

I'm black, therefore I'm not: this is what four hundred years
of errors and trials—faith wrung out from unripened rinds—
forced folks with the nerve to be born neither wealthy nor white
to know from the get-go. And for the love of a stained-glass God,
don't speak off-script or they'll wash the mutiny from your mouth
with a firehose; that's why most men lie down mutely in darkness,
safe or at least sheltered, beneath the underdog of hatred & history.

Get them to kill each other, or even better, hoodwink them
into hating themselves: that's the anti-American Dream too
many citizens sleep through, fed a fixed diet of indifference,
intolerance, and interference. So what can you do if you know
you're a genius, and all the klan's men can never convince you
water isn't wet? Keep rolling that rock up the hill until it grinds
a fresh groove into the earth: improvise your own *force majeure.*

This is almost my time, he said, and good God wasn't he
more than half-right. I know one thing (you can quote him),
I'm not going to let anyone change me. Overflowing with
awareness of himself, fresh out of the furnace, molded in
the image of a bird that flew first and further—mapping out
the contours of this new language: dialogic, indomitable—
his work exploded, a defiant weed cutting through concrete.

1957: five albums in twelve months—righteous waves
quenching a coastline, reconfiguring the world the way
Nature does. And his reward—a brief stretch in Bellevue,
ain't that a bitch? Listen: when The Duke declared music
his mistress, he was lucky enough to need nobody, aware
that the genetic razor cleaving obsession and insanity is
capricious, like all those calamities Poseidon orchestrated.

Mingus was never not human, the impossible endowment
that drove him, destroyed him and, in death, restored him.
His tenacity was the heat that both healed and hurt, a comet
cursed with consciousness—he went harder, dug deeper,
even as his best work impended, yet-unrealized revelations:
Blues and Roots the brown man's burden, a thorny crown
worn only by dispossessed prophets willing or able to testify.

His recalcitrant wisdom: earned the way trees acquire
Rings—the reality of who he was, even if he too changed
at times, like the country that claimed him (mostly after
the fact). And whether you're committed, an exiled crusader,
or a respectable suit working to death in squared circles,
the message from that rare bird's song still resounds today,
an epiphany blown through the slipstream: *Now's the Time.*

Charlie Parker's Premonition

At least Bach believed in God—this is what saved him.
Can you fathom that freedom, the *peace* of such certainty?
In thrall to exigency, at once owned yet refusing ownership
of one's art. Accepting endowments that, on blessed occasions,
override routine; on hallowed days clamor for consummation
in a voice you alone are capable of divining, or better still,
chosen to channel: a commission you neither oppose nor suppress.

Sadly for the faithless, God's accessible only through transcription,
and often selects vessels not spiritually suited for the exchange.
How would you handle the hot urgency of some holy inspiration
if it awoke inside your mind, screaming like a starved exile?
Could you mitigate earthly debt in the sacred currency of psalms?
Or would you require synthetic unction to abide the consecration
of a million illimitable miracles—even if you scoff at such stuff?

Billie Holiday's Deathbed

(On May 31, 1959—as she lay dying at the Metropolitan Hospital in New York, aged 44—Billie Holiday was arrested, handcuffed, and put under police guard for possession of narcotics.)

This busy bee, at the end of a life like clockwork,
a symphony of service to everything but herself—
wings snatched in a world blinded by the way it is—
slowly expiring in the sweet nectar of silence, stung
with bittersweet poison, an alchemy of blinded faith.

And even this they could not abide.
Their white-hot burden, unappeasable,
like anti-gravity drawing light inside
its sense of self: righteous, obdurate,
enfeebled from all their inherited fears.

Who are these men that know nothing
about the blues? Inspiring jinxed history
with officious ink—corrections bled red
outside the margins, ignored or overcome—
their shared voice, warning: *Be more like me.*

Or worse still, *stay separate, apart, unheard;*
entitled or at least allowed to live: strange fruit
that rots inside dark spaces, or gets torn down
from trees, weeping their weary hymns of silence,
caustic smoke signals blown from burning crosses.

What do they know about beauty, their hatred the only thing
honest about them? What do they know about the helpless
ones: helpless for song, helpless for love, helpless for a fix,
helpless for joy, helpless for hope? God bless the child that
backward men would scorn, ignore, or erase—if they could.

Bud Powell's Brain

Was it that hard-boiled cop's unindicted Nightstick
that scrambled your system, sending misfired messages
into the soft-wiring that polices ungovernable impulses?

Or was collateral damage already done? Chemistry coalescing
the onset of sickness, like a chick pecking through its shell?

Uno Poco Loco: an epitaph for stillborn souls that can't
escape the yoke of adversity; Nature's always improvising,
uninterested in excuses, or anything that could plausibly explain
the roots of Squares—and circumstances of those serving them.

Poached forever by the eyes of the White and the Other
Color, printed in numbers on top of paper pyramids:
E Pluribus Unum—a private club you're forbidden entrance,
even decades after your death, a pitch black Ever After
that tastes and smells like vanilla extract and crackers, Jack.

This world's never been accommodating to hard cases, helpless
to understand languages they're confusedly fluent in, and
like a conjoined twin, it smothers thoughts and steals oxygen
from a disobedient brain, inflamed by anger or alcohol or
something stronger, risky antidotes for those inscrutable squawks
you'll transcribe for anyone, willing to open their ears
and better still, their wallets:
Fat fortresses dispensing the only justice
served after last call.

Something you can score, like love
or junk in any back alley.

Unless you can't
afford the going rate.
Which means, like always:
You're broke.

Howlin' Wolf's Arena

On occasion he would crawl across the stage,
not like a dog but a soldier trapped in a trench.

Avoiding sharp rim shots and blasts of brass or
the iced-over stares of bewildered civilians.

This, for him, was the front-line, something to abide
every night under those lights, and like any war,
it was more or less safe as the stretches of peace:

Wherein difference or friendly fire could kill you,
while the maître d', forever smiling, counted
the bodies, cleaned up, and served last call.

Sun Ra's Spaceship*

I'm not of this world, Ra insisted, and it was obvious
to everyone: He ain't one of us. You see, he swore, I am
from out there: I conjure up other worlds that could break your brain.
And to be Blount? This claim was only scarcely less credible
than faithful suckers talking to an old man in outer space.

Listen: magic's a trick when these cities are always the same,
suits suffocating fools and men calling you son, not Sonny—
an alien in their eyes—with black holes for hearts and their ears
stuffed with corn, that slop discreet folks covet for colorless meals,
when earthlings turn on machines to distract them from inner space.

(*Sun Ra (born Herman Poole Blount) was an American jazz composer and
bandleader. He adopted the name Sun Ra, claiming he was an alien from Saturn on
a mission to preach peace, and throughout his life he consistently denied any ties to
his prior identity.)

Liz Taylor's Talents

Apocalyptic, Richard Burton proclaimed.
They would topple empires, he insisted.

(And if that's not poetry, you can take all
the silicone from every centerfold,
and sell it to every dissolute purveyor
of pulchritude, going back in time
to Caesar, who knew a thing or two
about excess—and how to supervise
a spectacle or oversee the final cut.)

Tits are not unlike talents: you're born with them.
Of course, you can cultivate and refine and procure
all you want, Beauty's still in the eye of the Beholder.

As such, that lucky Dick immortalized
the archetype of an adoring gaze—as more than a handful
of prurient politicians or repressed priests
could ever fathom, with no quarter
or apology required for posterity.
Or especially what all those earnest but
wilted scribblers from a more Romantic Era
could convey, their sonnets smoldering
like moldy corsets in unread anthologies.

Joey Kocur's Fist*

Imagine a piano pounded to the point
where its ivory bones are chipped.

The black keys leaking blood
and exhausted from overuse.

Every note a raw rejoinder
perfected by pain and practice.

Each improvisation a stoic shriek
for the sake of the song.

(*Joseph George "Joey" Kocur is a former professional hockey player. He is best known as an enforcer with a devastating punch; he so frequently hit players with his right hand, often landing blows on their helmets or teeth, that his right hand was often in poor condition.)

Chef's Second Chance

"Never get out of the boat."   *--Chef, Apocalypse Now*

It never sat well that Chef, who endured so much
in the service of a suicide mission, found himself
smuggled as he slept, then sacrificed like a lamb shank—
collateral damage to the apocalyptic designs of Col Kurtz,
exterminating men with the carelessness of cooks, stewing
marbled meat until it sluggishly turns the color of steel pots.

So let's suppose, in a slightly less insane sort of world,
Chef gets a second chance. Stateside, run through the jungle
and back in his kitchen, taking orders even he can understand.
Ponytail in place, primed gently by grill grease and sweat,
a different cauldron altogether, head counts & tickets clocked
one plate at a time: straight wages for sensible work.

Except something is off: he can't break away from this place.
Not the job, but that unconquered country and the things he carries.
It couldn't break his will but it's slowly sucking on his soul,
his brain boiling with all he saw and can never not see.
The more he scrubs the less he shines (*Mistah Clean—he dead*).
Darkness stalking his heart, murdered babies beneath his boots.

Too many jobs lost to count, he's changed but nothing else did.
A survivor but nobody warned him about no shit like this:
His sins can't be forgiven. Fortunate sons smirk when he stands
at the bus stop, nowhere to go, no way to pay, so of course
cops come when he breaks down inside that bank, not trying
to hurt anyone, there's no gooks here and the gun's not even loaded.

(Over there I could empty a clip and get myself a medal;
ain't this a motherfuck! Five-to-ten for unlawful entry?)

So here you are. Came all this way and you finally get it.
Maybe you should have gotten your ass out of that boat.
The tiger was God trying to tell you a thing or two—too late,
you'll never know now—or else on a mission of its own:
finding you, afraid but still on your feet, some instinct
sending it up river to put you, at last, out of your misery.

Captain Ahab's Oil

He knew, somewhere deep within the bilious machinery
of an unburdened heart, that black money would mingle
with the bones and drowned souls of all his shipmates—
and himself. Ink spilled before it could begin unravelling:
all the visions and secrets of a thousand untold stories.

His commission, simply, to circle the Evil that hunted him
first, over oceans and across continents, avowed only to
the obscene spoils of revenge, an uncompromising conception:
Restitution—or else a reprieve—from the intolerable designs
of some remote deity, who torments everything He conceives.

To what end? A man's delegation, like any honest accounting,
wants exposition, *attainment*—the promise all authors make:
Follow and read what I've seen, bear witness to everything
I've endured. Of course, Ahab's enterprise assumed credulity
in the service of sin, accessories to the carnage he'd transcribe.

Great men often quell unquiet consciences with certainty:
in a cause or something appalling they've come to believe
is preordained, that grim force adjudicating earthly matters.
Thus, the sacrifice of those conscripted; the blood and blubber,
massed barrels brimming with dark proof of demons redressed.

And what of all the unused oil? Fuel that could feed families,
irradiate gloomy rooms, and compensate the keen industry
of those expendable hands on deck—driven by duty or else
more earthly matters: the typical costs subsistence extracts—
pliant men disinclined to resist such exorbitant sacrilege.

Himmler's First Blasphemy

Is it possible this psychopath had a sense of humor?

How else to account for those locales
he chose? Unsullied landscapes
unfit for grotesque deeds:
Assailing Nature's mise-en-scène.

Or did he believe
he was acting in accordance
with his whiter God's wishes?
Or worse, revamping the rough draft
of a divine architect—with infallible designs
but insufficient resources?

(The Almighty alone, with so many things
to contend with, each second something else
He was obliged to oversee or invent.

We don't, after all, judge geniuses
by scribbled notes left in drawers,
or the stalled progress of sketches
dropped on laboratory floors.

If not for the intrusions of bland men
with honorable intentions, the red ink
would be erased, a revised text enduring
as the permanent record. So

Successive generations would learn
differently, and revere these consecrated sites
where *difficult work* got done, inking
black & blue numbers on arms, defiling
the flesh, organizing bodies like so
many library books waiting to be
checked out.)

His aspersive vision: A new alchemy commissioned
by the uncorrupted hand of History.
A better future freed from abominations, begging erasure
from a distracted deity and stern disciples, willing to perfect,
at last, the little things He lamented not making
less defective—the first time
He tried.

Bill Cosby's Blindness

It's like the old joke about men having two brains,
or whatever ways male impulse and privilege have
forever been defined or denied, or else amalgamated.

He had appetites, certain types have always said,
whenever they wish to whitewash unsavory deeds
done in the disservice of others, without recourse.

Savor their gift, they also say, because nothing else
matters in the end, which is why wives and partners
and conquests are often, at best, asterisks in obituaries.

His mind, his heart, his *art*, all in the right place, right?
It was just his brain (you know which one) obliging him
to act in ways contrary to those better angels—and alibis.

Do what I say, not what I do is, of course, always there:
the script spoken during unfortunate aftermaths; it's hard
on men who are nothing if not instinctual beings—by design.

A TV street preacher using sit-coms and stand-up routines,
you caught so many flies in your filthy web, not man enough
to seduce or enthrall, but waylay, by Divine Right, your prey.

Not unlike a billionaire hustler hiding behind golden gates,
you cast subtle aspersions and got grandiloquent on
a congregation quick with its wallets and magnanimity.

Even while you whined about pound cakes and shilled
pudding pops, you refilled prescriptions, cheese for traps
you served in tainted cocktails: they drank and you defiled.

In the land of the blind, a man with *no* eyesight is king, or...
some shit like that; is this all you have to offer, at long last,
as you parade your pique, a penultimate, sorry performance?

Cast the first stone, some still say, despite everything
we've heard and seen from so many he tried to silence,
He's America's Dad, and look how his wife stands by him!

The same logical pretzels good masters employed, pretending
they were men of God with little ladies they were raising to rule
the world, even as they cleaned up dirty deeds and dirty drawers.

Side action's the collateral damage of men with desires & history's
routinely reconciled the ways our cultural heroes have victimized
the voiceless while they got busy, ardently reshaping our realities.

Hey Dr. Huxtable, at any point did it occur that you'd become Everything
you claimed to despise, but worse? Your trespasses all empowered
by prestige—and what only those with lost souls dare call prerogative?

Trayvon's Last Meal

Once upon a time, a teen, I stole
silver pieces from my mom's purse,
because I had a habit to feed—and
mostly it didn't matter because I *could*.

Every day, after school, candy of
every color; pimple bait only boys
who jerk off into dirty socks find
enticing, free to be ugly and dumb.

What I'm saying is I was unexceptional.

What is this? This guilt? Do memories carry
contriteness for every transgression, real or
especially imagined? Immunity's having dough
and the answers to questions never even asked.

If you were innocent what would you choose
for your last meal? The entitled—amendable—
might say bread which is life which is God...and
before dying see what is white and what is wrong.

Tina Turner's Legs

Those thighs could crack your back
like a peanut beneath a pair of pumps.
Or slice your head off like freshly-shaved
scissors, and you'd lick them like lollipops,
in awe and almost insane, a dream cum true.

No, video is good as it'll ever get—and
that's good enough: you wouldn't even
begin to know how to handle those miles
of succulent straight lines, lost in darkness,
delirious; look but don't touch or better
yet, just listen. There's a lot you could learn:

the thigh bone's connected to the hip bone,
the hip bone's connected to the back bone...

Look at them. Walk a mile in those heels:
Muscle and rhythm and the brutal love
of harmony. You have to be strong to bear
that body of work. You carry that weight
long enough and the burden becomes a kind
of blessing, at least in the eye (and especially
the shy, shaking hands) of the beholder.

Take a deep dive into this river and come
out on the other side of the mountain, high.

We always try to kill what we can't control;
that's a whole history of colored commentary.

Black and blue, the blackened blues of beautiful blackness.

Listening and looking, thirsty like a lush
in a liquor store, but this kind of sweetness
could kill you—and you'll die tasting brown
sugar on your tongue, panting like Pavlov's
bitch, kissing those soles, holding out hope
that one day soon they'll walk all over you.

Jimi Hendrix's Hair

Would one single strand, swept off stage left, reveal
the mysteries of existence, or at least unlock the magic
of your mind, all sixes and nines, gypsy eyes, footprints
dressed in red, mirrored rooms, and belly button windows?

Were those drops of sweat acid-laced, doused by gods
in lab coats, or were uncanny causes in play—Voodoo
Soup—transmissions from a halo of ashes and inspiration?

Are we even meant to fully fathom the conception of all these
colors—without names, without sounds—content some amongst
us are selected, and given voice to an intelligence alien to our ears?

Did everything you did happen so fast we scarcely saw it, or are we
still grasping at this electric air—midnight lighting and light years
of secrets and equations that we, for lack of other options, call Art?

Jake LaMotta's Rage

A boxer's fury must be cultivated, surely.
But the best ones are fed the same way
as silent calves enclosed in iron pens:
the grain funneled by force, a practice
perfected by centuries of risk vs. reward
and, always, money. Through this process—
capricious but productive, with perfect specimens
churned out like the livestock they are—choking
as they must on what they're made to swallow,
fed for precision and a finite time to thrive
before an abrupt and brutal abrogation (the only
merciful thing they'll ever experience), any fighter's
endgame in reverse: an ever-after orgy for those senses
deprived for so long, all in service to a science
that starts sweetly than sours, ostensibly overnight.

Broken down and no longer especially useful,
bruised fists soaking in filthy ice, scarred eyes surveying
the opposite corner of an empty ring, they're put out
to pasture but not out of their misery: they endure,
bodies imploding and fury boiling like a red cape,
a recipe or reason for choler that can no longer be quelled—
if ever was—the taste for blood bred early, now
instinctual, and fighting (others, oneself) the only thing
a warrior can do. Only now one's wrath isn't measured
in three-minute increments; can never be sated with
sex or booze, feasts or pills, life itself a split decision.

Alone (again or at last) in a widening field,
this bull raging in a new arena, the fix in
and the only currency everything he's had
beaten into him, every ticking second a mockery
and reminder: you may the Boss for a minute but
another boss made this world before it made you.

Private Pyle's Pain

You think soap bars in a towel
hurts? Physical pain is fleeting,
and scars on skin heal quicker
than a soul broken by a band
of brothers—with darkened hearts,
trained to adapt and endure, born again
harder than anything you ever
imagined, back in a home town
where guns killed only for food,
when you could eat when hungry
and sleep soundly, safely; unable to
imagine monsters under your bunk
bearing arms against you, disrupting
dreams where baby-faced boys despair
about all the things we have to destroy
inside ourselves, in order to survive.

Kurt Vonnegut's Cigarettes

So it goes. There's only one thing you can rely on, but don't
think about that Hocus Pocus; the artistry of our inhumanity.

And our absurd genius at inventing novel ways
to slaughter, or worse still, erase all evidence of everyone
not born with ways and means inherited, cultivated
by History that renders errors invisible by magic, acts
required so that otherwise silly people are taken seriously, or else
It's back to the drawing board, where epitaphs are immortalized
amongst the rubble, after solutions are finalized, silenced witnesses
smoked out by the one Deity everyone must obey: Death.

What is about smoke and death, anyway? Remember the way
they sold us things, like crusades and cigarettes or stakes
made to cleanse and clarify brutal truths, rare and bloody,
marinated in words every minister or mother knows by heart:
This hurts me more than it hurts you, no matter what

Your eyes tell you: adjourn judgment and go with your gut,
the capacity to discard childish things, like Love over Loyalty.

God wrote a book of His own, you see; the writing on the walls
of every cemetery and formal institution. Ask no questions and
it will all make sense if you make it to eternity, all the injustice
and contradiction that bedevil the ones caught in the crossfire—

Which is everyone, you've seen. So? If you still can't comply,
how about going to sleep in your garage, or else try something
a bit more brazen, say, a belt tightened around your Adam's apple?
Or eat a bullet, the Breakfast of Champions, or belly flop
off a bridge? Or admit you're not man enough to be a man
of action, they whom appall those who think thinking is salvation.

No, you know, despite all the unspeakable things you've described,
there's only one alternative: practice what you preach, soldier
on, pretending paradise isn't lost if enough of us say *Enough*.

And pray that Truth sticks to us like Time, that's there's not Nothing
after the ending of every story ever told, every illusion entertained,
every entreaty unanswered, a snuffed-out pile of Pall Malls—those
friends who always tell you straight: you're dying so why not enjoy it?

Beethoven's Silent Consecration

Darkness.
Too much like death?
No, too much like *life*.

This not-quite-nothingness:
an adagio
separating suffering
and self.

Recalcitrant; composing.

Conceiving entire orchestras
craving illimitable expression.
Sound: some sacred requital.

The snow, falling softly
outside, effulgent—
every flake a separate
note, each expressing
its own song.

Silence?

Dreaming of death:
a prolonged peace.

Seeing people seeing
and hearing, knowing
this music will speak
when even speech, finally
fails him.

Richard Pryor's Flesh

Take, eat; this is my body which is broken for you...
(How many times did we hear that, back in the day?)

This cup is the new covenant in my blood...
(In remembrance of Who? Which Way Is Up?)

The light shines in the darkness...
(Do you see the light?)

And the darkness has not overcome it...
(Lead us not into temptation.)

But deliver us from Evil...
The church was our school and vice versa, both
things we outgrew as we grew out of everything
they beat into us. So many switches swinging
in the winter wind, breaking our backs because
this hurts you more than it does me, thy will be done.

Cast them into the furnace of fire—now we're talking.
Every man who tells the truth has to take the heat:
Face it, eat it, bathe in it, and pour lighter fluid
on the flames—this is just what a genius does.

Sacrifice him there as a burnt offering...
You see, the gods demand abnegation, their alms.
Mere mortals can put cash in the basket,
but certain sorts of men pay a different way—
the kind of currency that leaves singed skin
and scars: that's the price of admission.

When you walk through the fire, you will not be burned...
How? Bodies are only boats, surrounded by the spirits.
Why? If you have to ask you'll never know.
Prove you mean it, *that* means you're real.
This life only hurts because you're alive.

Ornette Coleman's Question

Imagine if entire realities could burst into being,
fully formed like perfect rows of grain—the same
way an artist's sweat dissolves into air, is subsumed
by clouds that grow pregnant and explode: this torrent
of water soaking the soil; a ceaseless, restorative cycle.

Sonny Rollins's Bridge*

It wasn't *his* bridge, of course.
It wasn't even his city, and it certainly wasn't
his world. It's *your* world, jazz music says,
I'm just living in it. And the world's a workshop.

Sonny was different, though. Even for one
we'd call young gifted & black without being
bromidic. Sonny heard so much but mostly
only listened to himself, waiting and creating
his own kind of way, expressing everything.

How do we describe the kind of man already
in rarified air deciding he wasn't high enough
(having already eschewed the artificial ecstasy
that ruins veins and soils brains, Body & Soul)?

This colossus, keeping his own council, split
his apartment to set up shop in the crow's nest
of the Williamsburg Bridge, perhaps the one
place aside from the Arctic Circle where no one
could see or hear history being picked apart
like a carcass, and then reassembled in real time.

Three years of this. Almost a thousand days
while the world spun, the cash registers rung,
and so many pretenders to the throne ascended
for lack of better options. Sun turned to snow
and dawn turned to dark and there were still
all those sounds: a style being tweaked, a gift
being refined, an experiment being improvised.

The quest for vision, it's said, will make
otherwise steady men see outlandish sights:
as they deprive themselves of human fuel
they become something at once less & more
than a vessel; the spirits speak to and through
them and once that barrier is broken, one sees
oneself changed, then begins changing the world.

(*In 1959, feeling pressured by his unexpected rise to fame, Rollins took a three-year hiatus to focus on perfecting his craft. A resident of the Lower East Side of Manhattan with no private space to play, he took his saxophone up to the Williamsburg Bridge to practice alone.)

Roland Kirk's Dream

It appeared to him, he said, while he slept.

Or, rather, it revealed itself to him, the way
visions will, seeming nonsensical to those
who claim to see—the light in their eyes
conveying what they believe is required
of them—no revisions necessary for this
rough draft we're born into, a book with
backward pages or pictures upside-down.

(What if you could train your brain to talk
through instruments, creating dialogues
out of time or space: sound that surrounds?

Are creatures in the darkness of the deep,
or farthest out in stellar regions, sightless?
Or do they perceive what nothing else can
process, forsaking the cues and clues given
to brothers and sisters slower on the uptake?

Are they blind or do they *see* differently?
Do our eyes watch—or just reinterpret all
they're told, wires pulled behind the seen?)

Kirk's work shifts things, realigning reality.

This is music that says: I was here, I am alive,
we don't die when we're no longer here; we are
dark stars bringing light for those who can prepare
themselves to deal with miracles, where art becomes
like armor, protecting and serving, and if too often
it falls on deaf ears it *stays* made, gets heard, remains
unreal in the ways that matter most: bright moments
or an inflated tear exploding—like a dream deferred.

Eric Dolphy's Death*

If ever there was a time for some Deus ex machina
it was there, in that alley; angels instead of uniforms
finding you, half-asleep—on your way somewhere else.

But perhaps sacred spirits don't intervene in the affairs
of their messengers, and there was nothing any of us stuck
here on earth—busy as ever not saving ourselves—could do.

(*In 1964 Dolphy, who suffered from undiagnosed diabetes, collapsed after a
gig in Berlin and fell into a coma. The attending physicians, as was typical of
the times, wrongly assumed this black musician had overdosed, and left him
alone to sleep off the effects of the drugs. Dolphy, a teetotaler, neither drank nor
took drugs, as a simple blood test would have affirmed.)

Booker Little's Deliverance*

Your blood, poisoned by neither drink nor drugs,
but the ravening appetite of some fickle force
we can't fathom; the way hearts attack us or else
our systems are assailed by cells made to invade.

At least fate had the courtesy to inquire if you had
any final words: your short life's work summarized
on two albums that scorn mortality, even as death
circled your ailing body like a demented buzzard.

Strength and sanity, victory and sorrow—
calling softly: holding a lantern, showing
us some of what you were already seeing.

Was this expression—an elegiac storm still able
to inspire and console, capable of changing lives
half a century after it got stuck to magnetized tape;
just another day in the studio, that odd laboratory
of mournful miracles—worth all it took to make?

Those revelations transmitted from the impassive edge
of elsewhere, a place memory and deed are annihilated:
some insatiable absence of being where all sound ceases.

(*Booker Little, a virtuosic composer and trumpet player, died tragically at 23 due
to complications from uremia. Prolific during his abbreviated career, Little managed
to lead two influential sessions in 1961, despite being in considerable and constant
pain.)

John Coltrane's Cancer

Coltrane's calling: all he did was *everything*
in his power, throwing sparks at the darkness,
extolling what he alone conceived—the Divine
Alchemy of his own design, sheets of sound
with no barriers between pursuance, his spirit,
and interstellar space, this gift a supreme kind
Of Love.

But like some indefatigable oyster, filtering
the sins from a fathomless sea, he transformed,
instigating storms no human being can contain.
And like any authentic prophet, with fire cloaked
as expression, every revelation must supersede
the messenger, even mortality, ever insatiable as
It Is.

And so, those bilious juices grew emboldened,
their corrosive wake drowning him in everything
he tried not to be, leaving him earthbound and
anchored, even as his soul strained, relentlessly
toward infinity. And death, etiolated in the end,
silenced him much as a passing shadow consumes
The Sun.

Shafi Hadi's Silence*

i.

Those sounds, not falling on enough ears
then. Inaccessible, unknown, unwanted—now.

Today, where audiences vote for winners
hand-picked by specialists called consultants and
marketing departments with both barrels aimed
beneath the bottom line, a nothing-in-common
Denominator for something once considered sacred:
Art. Or was it something else altogether, something
important? Jazz was actually a matter of life and death—
Beautiful but always too short: the note, the feeling,
the connection, the song, the show, this life.

Made in America: a way to relate invented
by the people, for the people, for sale, forever.

Because it was meant to last it could never last,
at least long enough to survive our obsession for
new things, and the old-fashioned notion of
interests and attention spans longer than shadows,
cast quietly in a smoke-soaked nightclub.

ii.

Who did we become? Over-rehearsed and under-employed,
outcast or worse, obscure enough to not warrant a second
look: unrecognized in familiar places no one knows about
Or bothers to go because nothing happens there anymore.

Where did we go? Into used record bins and basements,
burn-outs or bums, teachers or else repurposed as working
stiffs, at offices or in asylums or out on the streets, the ones
who knew they were never going nowhere:

Tripping always over those sticks and stones that
kept us high and put us under the earth,
slings & arrows of outrageous misfortune: all
the effort, all the energy, all the discipline, all for nothing.

What did you think? We could eat the air and drink up
the Nothing like nourishment? No, it was sketchy enough
when we looked into the dark and lit eyes looked back at us:
Two-drink minimums and overpriced appetizers keeping
the front of the house solvent for a few more evenings.

Even then we shuffled & scrapped and kept hoping that
these works-in-progress—also called our lives—would
mean enough to enough of you that we could keep
the act intact, long enough to do something more than survive.

Or else avoid seeing the light that meant everything was
over: the gig up, the profits gone, the sounds expired.

iii.

What the hell, I say, the world never owed none of us
a living, and who said anyone should feel sympathy
for men making sounds no one asked to hear?

For solidarity with a handful of humans exploring
the spaces in between us and what we used to call
the underground: that backstage some are born into,
asking, *Are great artists born or made?* Or else:

Who cares? The best ones find their way, always, or
get found, discovered, rescued, rehabilitated even
after they die. But what about the ones left behind
The seen? The ones keeping the beat or blasting
their melody, the ones on the front lines behind
the man, side-men no one would know, in the grooves
or on the bus. How could you say you know me
when I don't even know myself? No more time,
no more chances, no more luck, no more life.

So when do we go? Is it that same old song
and dance with Death? The unhappy ending all of us
nod off to, humming some tired tune when time's up and
the band plays on—all around us—while we stumble or stretch,
happy, blind, scared, or sensing something sort of like bliss,
into the dark? Is it, in the end, the opposite of that sound

we spent a lifetime learning and playing and loving and lamenting?

The one sound we all reckoned would still linger
after the last encore of the greatest show on earth:

Silence.

(*Saxophone player Shafi Hadi, born Curtis Porter, is best-known for his association with jazz legend Charles Mingus, and played on the seminal recording Mingus Ah Um, from 1959. He dropped out of the scene in the early '60s and the reasons why, and his current whereabouts, are unknown.)

Henry Chinaski's Horses

He couldn't face the words, he wrote,
until he made it back from the track.

For a man famous for his refusal
to use metaphors, telling it straight like a tire iron,
this one kind of crept up on him, like they do.

Sort of the way the so-called real world punches suckers.

But perhaps that's still too affected by half, since
the only thing, we know, worse than too little
Truth is too much of the same old shit.

Anyhow, Hank had his horses and his handicaps,
like all of us, no matter what we tell ourselves.
Whether it's humping a desk or hustling the Morning Line,
or finding other ways to avoid assenting to work
altogether, we all need patterns and schemes.

Because by regulating our routines, they free up aspects
of ourselves—otherwise unengaged, like our dreams and
imaginations:

Or else we're out of time, out of our minds.

So, Hank had his horses and they told him who he was
on any given day: a winner, a loser, a player—and blinkered
or busted or flush, he returned to his humble post position and
that typewriter, waiting for him and placing its own bets:

Was the master in form? Pulling up lame? Wielding his whip?
Could he coax them through the muck, past the front of the pack?
Ending with the ultimate trifecta: booze and women and words.

(Then pause for a money shot, parading past the Winner's Circle.)

Success is a salve that quenches a cultivated kind of thirst, and
what matters, finally, isn't how you walk through the fire, but
the resolve to put your feet forward in the first place,
urging all those ideas to sneak up like solved secrets:

Reminders that even Long-Shots need somewhere to go,

Some way to live.

Sean Murphy has been publishing fiction, poetry, reviews (of music, movie, book, food), and essays on the technology industry for more than twenty years. He has appeared on *NPR's* "All Things Considered" and been quoted in *USA Today, The New York Times, The Huffington Post, Forbes,* and *AdAge.* A long-time columnist for *PopMatters,* his work has also appeared in *Salon, The Village Voice, Washington City Paper, The Good Men Project, Memoir Magazine,* and others. He has been nominated for the Pushcart Prize two times, once for short fiction and once for poetry. His poems have been widely anthologized, including the collections *Revisiting the Elegy in the Black Lives Matter Era, This Is What America Looks Like, Lo-Fi Poetry Series: Poet Sounds, and Written in Arlington: Poems for Arlington, VA.* The author of a memoir, novel, and two collections of non-fiction, he has completed his first collection of short fiction and is working on a second collection of poems. He was previously the writer-in-residence at Noepe Center for Literary Arts at Martha's Vineyard. He's Founding Director of 1455, a nonprofit organization seeking to advance the appreciation of and passion for the literary arts through programs that support expression, education, and the sharing of writing and literature, based in Winchester, VA. As a former analyst for the technology industry, he wrote extensively about the ways an increasingly digital reality is changing lives, not always for the better. These essays and articles inspired his podcast *The Intersection of Innovation and Culture,* which focused on the ways technology, despite its inherent contradictions, has undeniably democratized content and provided a more inclusive environment for creative endeavors. At 1455, Murphy has established the bi-monthly publication *MOVABLE TYPE,* and curated The 14:55 Interview series, which features writers and artists discussing their work, their influences, and what inspires them. Sean lives in Reston with his wife Heather and their three dogs.